T0160770

Methodist Hatchet

Methodist Hatchet

Ken Babstock

poems

ANANSI

This edition published in 2011 by
House of Anansi Press Inc.
110 Spadina Avenue, Suite 801
Toronto, ON, M5V 2K4
Tel. 416-363-4343
Fax 416-363-1017
www.houseofanansi.com

Distributed in Canada by	Distributed in the United States by
HarperCollins Canada Ltd.	Publishers Group West
1995 Markham Road	1700 Fourth Street
Scarborough, ON, M1B 5M8	Berkeley, CA 94710
Toll free tel. 1-800-387-0117	Toll free tel. 1-800-788-3123

House of Anansi is committed to protecting our natural environment.
As part of our efforts, the interior of this book is printed on paper made from
second-growth forests and is acid free.

16 15 14 13 12   4 5 6 7 8

LIBRARY AND ARCHIVES CANADA CATALOGUING IN PUBLICATION

Babstock, Ken, 1970–
Methodist hatchet / Ken Babstock.

Poems.
ISBN 978-0-88784-293-1

I. Title.

PS8553.A245M48 2011   C811'.54   C2010-906476-3

Library of Congress Control Number: 2010940726

Cover design: Bill Douglas
Typesetting: Marijke Friesen

We acknowledge for their financial support of our publishing program
the Canada Council for the Arts, the Ontario Arts Council,
and the Government of Canada through the Canada Book Fund.

Printed and bound in Canada

Laura and Samuel

Contents

[   ]

The Decor

Comes a time we all must aspire, no?
      Magazines declaring
in big sans serif: *Style, Interior, Form,* and
      Chair. Ok, I invented
Chair, but glossy spreads depicting
outrageously beautiful rooms

wherein one diminutive, three-legged, teak,
      mid-century stool
with a triangular seat and nubby
      cloth upholstery
of an unassuming meadow green
might very well cost

upwards of four grand. *Those* magazines.
      To the right of the chair
on the floor, a pile of stacked art books:
      Cindy Sherman, say,
Brice Marden, Gerhard Richter —
a Max Frisch novella

splayed on top like a stone bird on a plinth.
      I know, reading
the spines, I've entered into a kind of silent
      exchange
with the — what — art director? Nothing
now eases the buzzing

suspicion I'm being signalled to from across
        a great distance,
as in semaphore, or prayer. Someone
        wearing a Tag Heuer watch
swivelling behind a desk
in New York, or London,

wants very badly to trigger in me a visual
        of earned leisure in idealized
surroundings.
        Surroundings
that better describe how I'd already
long been picturing myself.

"It is not easy to write a familiar style"
        as Hazlitt had it. Then who
doesn't "hate to see a load
        of band-boxes go along
the street?" Corian slab in the calibrated
cubism of the kitchen,

brushed nickel, much is re-stressed, salvaged
        hangar door, its blast-
shadow of early corporate logo, laminate's
        blue-black is Reinhardt-deep,
a Chiclet gleam. Lucite "ghost chair"
blocking a view of chalk

petroglyphs. And isn't to picture oneself to mimic
        the distant highway
grader, slugging off toward rural anomie,
        appearing not smaller but
farther away, spitting at cattle, leaning
into work, overtaken and

honked at. Is this about style? I remember being
       warned ontology was ugly
by a poet who then ordered the chowder. Grass
       tells a story of listening
to Social Democrats and de-mobbed
Wehrmacht scrap it out

deep in a post-war mineshaft, headlamps
       casting flattened
versions of their huddle up against gouged
       rock wall, or ascending
cage panel, up toward sun-licked rubble, civic
life utterly fucked, but

somehow on the mend — That's a different
       magazine. My girlfriend
and I went halves on a chair and sofa set.
       Mid-century, yes, but knock-offs.
Nubby green upholstery, though
a green less meadow

than that mineral-rich, polyethylenized
       turquoise the Inside Passage
reflects seen from a ferry rail sailing south
       from Prince Rupert
to Port Hardy. You can see straight
through it to more of it.

The chair became our older dog's day bed.
       She'd roll into a brindled
donut, or flip and act the otter, her legs
       in air, head dangled as
counterweight over the armrest. A month ago
she chewed through

the fabric, a hole you could slide an arm into.
        Slide an arm right through
the surface of this picture,
        into whatever spatial realm lies
behind the illusion of depth, to hold
the hand of the person

wanting so badly to be seen precisely
        as they feel themselves
to be: launching, from over there, starched
        murmurs, mere vibrations
of air, in hopes they can correct the distorted,
over-adorned version

they fear you've displaced them with. And
        have you? Can you
know, lost in the forest of what J.L. Austin
        dubbed "medium-sized
dry goods": the bang, the furniture
the olufsson and clutter of

the manifest image? Sea-Dog, Redbird, bottled
        schooner, bug husks.
The disconnected current gauge was a gift,
        its needle stilled between
"Reverse clips" and "Start charge." Consult it
and it shivers on a hash mark.

As Marginalia in John Clare's *The Rural Muse*

I wasn't finished. From as far back
as I can recall having heard a voice in my skull

I've wanted to die, or change, or die
changing. Hexagonal window, the moon

penned in it, and a segmented swarm sucking
up peonies. Heat off tar shingles

in June as the blood in one arm
blackened, thickened, went blearily toxic,

I exited earth up an IV tube.
The wall-mounted paper dispenser

narrating nightmares of scale, sores fell
from fingers — get well petals — and grew

back puce. Slug of little light, the bedrail
gleamed. Warmed yoghurt, a summons

button and visual aphasia. Now I've no spit,
no hospice and admit nothing, or,

for long stretches, only what happened
was all that ever could have happened.

Reeds curtain where land abuts lake,
if such limit exists, if ducks aren't taken

by pike mid-thought.

Carolinian (Crosscut with Sound)

Colander, canopy, colander. Contrivance
of green light-spots we're leoparded by.
Wild grape ampersand.

Joining land with how we see the land, walk softly
over the mudded impress shod horses
made earlier —

their dung looks fungal, very "forest floor."
Mid-trunk, one or more twig buds
whose cells continue to multiply

but never differentiate.
Atop a paper-bag groundcover,
tympany of deer deciding gone's best,

"patter of Delia's feet."
Burl Ives puns follow hard on the heels
of calling Kentucky blue timothy, and timothy

red fescue, and fescue not Kentucky
blue, not panic grass, but some kind of wheat.
None of it native and the six of us six

pages of *Murphy* or *Watt*.
Trail attendants made cordwood of the blowdown.
If we had growths that big we'd be televisually

famous. It's here the trail splits, loops back,
past the Z of a fawn's foreleg
portending not much from the black mulch,

to where squat cars are themselves slubs
on the bolt of horseradish field trimmed with purple phlox.
They'd shave or slice those monstrous,

boxed-ear excrescences to make Vermeer…
I mean, "veneer." I was back on the light.
Decorative veneer. It's so not quiet in here.

Autumn News from the Donkey Sanctuary

Cargo has let down
her hair a little and stopped pushing
Pliny the Elder on

the volunteer labour.
During summer it was all *Pliny the Elder,*
Pliny the Elder, Pliny

the — she'd cease only
for Scotch thistle, stale Cheerios, or to reflect
flitty cabbage moths

back at themselves
from the wet river-stone of her good eye. Odin,
as you already know,

was birthed under
the yew tree back in May, and has made
friends with a crow

who perches between
his trumpet-lily ears like bad language he's not
meant to hear. His mother

Anu, the jennet with
soft hooves from Killaloe, is healthy and never
far from Loki or Odin.

The perimeter fence,
the ID chips like cysts with a function slipped
under the skin, the *trompe*

l'oeil plough and furrowed
field, the UNHCR feed bag and restricted visiting
hours. These things done

for stateless donkeys,
mules, and hinnies — done in love, in lieu of claims
to purpose or rights —

are done with your
generous help. In your names. Enjoy the photo.
Have a safe winter

outside the enclosure.

Caledonia

Then we came out in numbers. Organized as Canadians
we came out in numbers with flags. With flags aloft

and hooting we stepped out in anger and in numbers. In
numbers as Canadians we came out drunk and threw rocks.

We threw rocks and golf balls as our patience had come to its
natural end. As Canadians we threw rocks past our flags aloft.

Having finally been angered enough we came out at night with
rocks. We'd been as Canadians infringed upon we thought

with flags. So we threw rocks. Rocks and choice epithets and golf
balls hooting. You don't live here we're proud Canadians in anger

with rocks and not limitless patience we appeared in numbers
around barrel fires and spoke. Into megaphones at the OPP drunk

and them we'd had enough of as Canadians. Citizens with flags
and megaphones and our rights and some of our children threw

rocks at the very end of their young patience with flags and placards
hooting. Our kids came out in numbers to stand in solidarity with

us into megaphones demanding we throw rocks and a few choice
Canadians without access to that road as our only route through

anger with flags aloft alongside placards and our kids angry to be
blocked by them with special treatment to be angered by rocks

thrown in Canadian solidarity with megaphones and our kids
in numbers aloft in a wind over patience our only route you don't

have to live near them as Canadians drunk with rocks. We came out
in numbers at night as Canadians around barrel fires singing.

West Range

Skyline cranes toward its source in cranes —
each demarcates a height
we urge the girders grow to; the girders might
just as well ignore us, though. Emily Haines

ignores the limits of her skin,
and molded plywood's not lumber,
but was. "Capitalism in December"
stands as subject of the poem and the ink

it's written in. Gondola, ferris wheel,
ex-urban angled dishes. Shiny, shiny Liebeskind.
This locust branch, up close, looks sequined
and particular. What *wouldn't* I prefer to feel

then feel at ease for having felt? Denver's
mostly cut glass in shops, ski slopes, Joe Sakic,
and a dull ache … You're reading this, or the inverse
is happening, while a collection of Schick

disposables grows mountainous in po-faced defiance
of its jingle. The best we can get. In finance's
long shadow
we'll one day bow

to men of higher station,
notice below us, in dark pools, our reflection,
like figures salvaged from a Caspar David Friedrich
but (was it Denver, or Jasper?) updated, in denim, freakin' rich.

Light Sweet Crude

A return to when Destroyer
        curled quiet in a corner of that rented room
waiting for the goat-white walls to shake.

In Prague they hear his *Rubies*
        as Gottwald's syphilitic blather, stashing
in their Pumas whatever it is Czech kids take.

Oh, to be rid of the rash,
        the rye, the redux, the relentless interiority!
No one occupies me like me. And no one

makes me lonelier. Universal
        compliance in the achievement of collective goods
is as much a fantasy as perfect competition.

Tin is ubiquitous. If I
        were a tin mine—ugly, sweating into the riverhead—
I'd look out on the world through the wheel

hubs of articulated truck
        beds and admit a paucity of spirit. My hole and ore.
My edge's ring road describing a spiral

divisible from space. Spirochete,
        nebulae. What's more he's self-taught, giddy
as Lautréamont, floating four feet above ground

running parallel to the unbuilt
        pipeline, singing Mine, baby, mine, baby, mine,
baby, all of it is mine. This time in the round.

Sugar Glider

— and when it was nervous or over-excited a noise,
maracas wrapped in mittens, lit
the room so the kids squealed and leaned
their heads into their neighbours' but
      with too much zeal or force; little Zizus

punctuating the epicentre of their lives' packed
stadium. Ah, friends; and friends
of animals. Life in the capital bulges vertically
and for the foreseeable future depends
      entirely on the continued safe disposal of crap,

such that were we to crown a plumber king,
she might reign with wisdom and forbearance
a very long while, leaving, like Marcus Aurelius,
some jotted *pensées* on the good sense
      of never getting too worked up about the plumbing.

For now, though, Barrie's not the worstest place
for a birthday party. Australia's inversion
of our Flying Squirrel — down there Toronto's
a suburb of Newcastle — makes an incursion
      into the fleecy vest of its handler as each rapt face

is the face of a clock in a shop in Bern or Annecy
only minutes into its revolution-headed-for-status-quo.
Sometime this month they'll find, or they won't,
what they've taken to calling the God particle. Moe,
      Frank, and Horst clogged the funding river so the LHC

very nearly didn't get built. Dark energy
is exuberance before language gets syntaxed. *Guhdeye, g'deh,*
Gadamer, giddy little monsters hopped up on sugar
and kissing indiscriminately. Away
        goes mercury in fur. Enter, the Flemish Giant, *Marjorie.*

Second Life

I left the north. I travelled south.
I got confused, I killed a horse.
I can't help the way I feel.
                        — The Smiths

So this is it, then. The party's more beautiful
perched Socratically, armed with chilled Pinot
Gris, unstapling Toronto's traffic
congestion, trading compliments, and pissing
themselves. You're at the fishtank,

fraternizing with the anemone. Fool. All of you
watched 40 donkey in through the service door,
yet only a week yesterday you committed
the delicate four-in-hand to memory, and
have still to feel your particulars

punched like braille into the plastic of credit.
Perhaps the leather wingtips are timeless, like
your inner life. Something in common with
the demographic pie-slice blue-ing in the middle
class. It gets centre stage, again,

cawing out a choral number about being nice,
up to a point. At the coat check a cute
Marxist hands over your keys, Clomid, sport jacket,
and happily discredited lineage, so leaving's
like arriving, with adjustments

for temperature. Ice-lights of the unbuilt city
visible through cable web and wrapped scaffold.
You can buy things. Speculate — though the word
needs defining. But in a gay club four doors
south, a young man's shaking it

and will, for hours, upright and fantastically
ripped, and courted by three others, badgers
to know where he's going afterward. Here's
the avatar, then, of an RL body crimped, bent,
volitionally stripped by cerebral

palsy, touch-typing in his folks' basement, telling
the live lens he loves "being someone other than me.
Someone who can dance and meet guys and feel
happy." Cut-glass magpie over the chipped nut dish,
heavy brocade, state pennants.

Galaga's now nostalgiaga for a simpler real, lateral
slide, single trigger button. It wasn't you in there
but your reflection chewing its tongue in the
plexi-glass. Money's the more virtual virtual —
I don't talk this way in Real Life.

Lee Atwater in Blowing Snow

Strangely, things sharpen visually,
gather mass into themselves, hugging colour as though
their own physical limits were arms. I

haven't expressed it well, but spruce
in this park shoot skyward yet settle into a loaded, over-ripe
ur-green set off against the new, white,

puffed-up second tree each tree's
acquired. Fire hydrant in its bonnet and fox stole only glows
more vibrant gold and sits still. Every

humped thing plotting the graph of itself;
silent accumulation of secondary facts all pertaining
to a horizontal axis. The die-cast, bolted,

public bench, for instance, more comfy
now, with padded slats, though no one sits there. The waist-high
commemorative plaque's just another

memory beneath a growing drift.
It looks like cake. What I like is the blunt foreknowledge
of gusting head winds. Pick out

the advance edge of a gathering front
from some distance off, ghosted surf, harridan's skirt. Like
footage of a cloud of krill, or shoal

of silver fish, the white points stall mid-air
then alter course, shift, re-align and gather speed all synced
to a system, signals not audible to us.

Coleridge saw starlings flit and sweep
then climb and bank en masse and thought his mind resembled
them, kept him from finishing great

things he'd long ago begun. It wasn't
the opium. Shadows bloom, stretch, cat-paw across the blank as
a surfeit of you; spillage, black dew.

The Living Text

He fell into an incinerator and was let out by drunks —
I listened harder as C. talked, leaning into the scrum
to catch what came next. Re-reading Pinsky's
Dante that day, here was the usual social hum

clarifying, resolving, into a modern re-telling of one
of the early circles. *He'd stacked the pickup with gyproc,*
warped studs, splintered laths, whatnot, and gone
out around 3. He said he'd get pasta, oatmeal, and milk

from the Ultramar after so I wasn't missing him yet
when the pickup came back but driven by buddy who'd
opened the iron hatch from the outside. Bets
went up over whether he'd cooked it, brewed

up a vat of bullshit to bring back to the city, enlisting
C. in the telling so he could pan across, fully
enjoy from a distance, the looks of astonishment, the ring
of gullible, dove-cheeked, city friends' faces. *He'd*

positioned himself above it, on the downward slope
heaving stuff into its core when the oven erupted, flared up,
and he turned to look down in — his foot lost an edge
in the scree and the next thing he's clung to a ledge

inside *the machine.* The slipknot of visuals began to undo.
What we couldn't imagine actually happening had,
and to see it we'd need facts, numbers, one or two
scale diagrams outlining events, signed in the hand

of the guy who, though drinking, had witnessed M. trip,
watched from his truck past the dump from a height.
When she'd finished narrating, someone started to clap
in his direction as though a near miss had occurred right

there in that room, or he'd announced he'd climb in the oven
to reappear from the sink-drain. *He'd been in four minutes.*
Four minutes of close-to-unbearable, untended smelter
with no apparent exit and all the air sucked out. Like tercets.

Something taking shape foggily about what Now is,
or might be: Plato's cave of riveted plate metal
set in the lee of a headland at the heart of a landfill,
a narrative bounced off our neighbours we memorize

together and re-tell to others to fill up some hours,
an undifferentiated noise-cloud words weep from
at intervals. *The fella who saw it, who saved him, swears*
it was nothing. An outline. Some sparks. A break from the rum.

A painter friend spritzed my aggrieved look with THC
in aerosol form. Medicinal. Mint-tinged. If there'd been
a thread I let go of it then, reclined under the halo of a GBV
record to therapeutically stroke the ears of a Lab of thirteen

who watched the rapt assembly disperse and dance. Skeptic
near the bean dip prodding veracity, *Wouldn't your eyes*
melt? as my own reddened, welled up. *We're going back*
in June to re-enact it. Film it. He's his own stunt double. The axe

of a migraine took my head off at the neck. Rock melted to fado.
I don't know who was leading, only we were led. Pale busts,
faces of strangers surfaced like koi in the oily kitchen window.
Dunno, you tell me is he different. This happened on the coast.

Which Helmet?

With the glove on, her pixellated breast every
demonstrably offensive line about young plums
and buds budding. With the glove and helmet on, "her"
is a proposition. With the helmet on she likes it when I
read to her from the book of desires I wrote
with the helmet on. Under the glove and helmet,
day indiscernible from night and want from love.
The other helmet cues God whispering in his quadrant.
There's no visor or need of one on the God helmet;
face a mask of contemptuous ecstasies, road
map of heaven on earth and the helmet on.
There's a crash helmet and infantry helmet
over in the corner that no longer fit as the head
of the poem has developed macrocephallicly.
Our universe, said to be coming apart at the seams,
poorly made, a *Jofa* from the mid-eighties, placing
us, like Butch Goring's head, at no small risk.
Jousting viable with the helmet on with the helmet
on time soups finally and selves sift. Horizons converge
in the mouth under the helmet and the glove
grips them like floss. This is Helmut Lang; I got
it at a consignment store. There's a Spartan
helmet behind glass; there's not much on it.
The helmet you were born
with very nearly obsolete, its list of incompatible
attachments growing longer by the day. Take trees,
for instance. Think of all the songs. Think of all the songs

without a helmet on and how they seem to weep
torrents over nothing for no reason. Put this on. Put
this on feel time die bewildered, binary, purchased
but no purchase gained, drainage
streaming out over the chinstrap.

Five Hours in St. John's

What would you do? Turns out your flight's not
till five, and your plate's been licked clean
since ten. Along Water St. the harbour-
facing shopfronts glaze under the heatlamp

of winter light. No one you know is here anymore.
The B&B hostess guarding your carry-on, despite
the room having slid into another guest's name.
Left to your own devices — the ones you reverse-

engineered from the grim sight of a motherboard
re-purposed as Frisbee by three kids and
their dog in a Winnipeg rail-yard — you'll operate
at a loss. March, a wind is up, the view

from Signal Hill contracts to your own face
turning wiper-fluid blue, colour-field study
in grey to the east, as your pulse slows to once
every other Ice Age. So, no. Up Temperance

onto Ordnance. Military Road. It's how things
go, sadly. Duckworth, Duckworth, surplus value
goose. Name the shades the siding's painted?
Tanning bed addiction, lilac-in-drag, recalled

Hershey's product, salt-flavoured bubble gum,
dawn of the trans-human age, flag of Guam
or Bahrain, tinned ham. Light green. Marginal
Wharf, then, to unravel the relational

web at the intersect of nautical and industrial
regress, "Morning! Um, what are the cranes
for?" "For keeping grip of the crates
when the city plunges eight feet." "Are you all

stevedore?" "Go on ye stunned bugger." "Yes b'y."
"No really. Go away." Shipping's no longer
an attractive proposition; these boats are ugly.
The Russian trawler, *HOBbIN CBET*, needs

paint, and the *Atlantic Concord*'s filling her
hold with shrink-wrapped pallets of collapsed
cardboard. Wanted, content provider. Prospect
St. is short and dim. Seed of Glory-fits, Bay-wop

made good, I stops in at Leo's chippy for a bite
and a think: moratorium cod, please,
heavily battered, with a side order
of slaw and fabricated nostalgia. No drink.

Irving station's Hopper shadows elongate
as the price per gallon ticks upward. The sky's
a recombinant number set of 7's, 4's, 3's
and 6's, but mostly 7's, their jittery pilots

following earth's great circles or gannet routes
or just input from Gander to wherever
the world is. They'll be back. As tourists,
or emergency groundings. For

The Bubble in the harbour to serve as Eliotic
correlative you have to work backward
to locate the subjective tone. Like the gulls,
you can smell it, and know there's detritus

afloat worth thieving, but its regnant property
might be described as flux and is really
just the shapes waste makes. Unsightly
but can be chalked up to local colour.

Finch called this the most un-self-conscious
of western cities. So what am I doing here?
Inhaling fumes, avoiding the cod-cakes,
wandering into the Marine Archives to pore

over floral print wallpaper, wind roses and berg
limits. The blow's cut with aspirin and talc,
unreported soft crime rates in Mt. Pearl
are up. I wish Steve Earle would come back,

his wire frames, mandolin and stricken
conscience. A sudden wind rakes NW, panics
the trout pool in Bowring Park, tugs
the sprayed hair of the weeping beech,

a beech well-known for being two trees grafted
into one. The gnarled bulge of a years-old scar
midway up. Never open a flick-knife
in a poncho with one eye on the pole star.

St. Anselm and Goods in Transit

That this sun, planed off the plank of horizon, divest itself of
riches beginning at the spectrum's richer, yellow end

*

That in their infinite   "Always"

*

That through our progeny course rivers of corn of corn of corn

*

That in that room with him were professionals, primary care-givers,
advocates in sheepskin coverlets passing an amulet and intoning

*

That regions of lesser average family income appear greyed in and
shipping wieners

*

That if not us some agent exercise a right to privacy independent
of such

*

That the blue-white range might wash or flood nothing more
sterile Dan Flavin could imagine

*

That razed acreage unearth PVC piping, arrowheads, unearth
plover eggs, a monk's cowl, unearth a predicate, unearth more
earth

*

That junk space expand to annex breakfast nook, nave, dropped
ceiling, nursery, neighbourhood

*

That manifest physically under diagrammed pyramid and stacked
cube *as* pyramid and stacked cube

*

That migrant labour, geese, hard red spring, nothing be imagined
that isn't a function

*

That distribution that suppliers that from which oceans altered
consuming by container-load

*

That suffused. Shot through. Inhering in cereal prices

*

That moreso even than bonobos can self-regulate, observed
intention in basic language games at levels a three-year-old in
Rosedale

*

That face time in aisle nine blue tunic under blue waves in a wrist-
brace on the ladder's fourth rung

Methodist Hatchet

> It was too much of a good thing
> but at least it's over now. They are making a pageant out of it,
> one of them told me.
> — John Ashbery

I read it somewhere — the derisive
tag the antecedents half-earned scowling at naked wallboards
when yet they clustered

on their dehiscent jut of oily granite.
In the demographic lacunae between the Catholic settlers of Salvage
and Sandy Cove's low Anglicans,

we *glory-fits, swaddlers*, we *Wesleyans*
counted as hypocrites, Janus-faced, joyless, pulpit-pounding cult
members with hypertension. Split

wood with one, you're alternately
cleaving air. Axe acting the middler to a Christmas spruce is the axe
shaving off a switch

then notching belt leather. Blade
above the goose's neck bisects the flecked, lashless, hazel sun
like a corneal scratch.

Tired weight — hear it? — like wet
gabardine, of barking on about moon-dogs' relation to the flight
path of a shrike, rhetoric's

murres, punishable life, the eddying
surface where potheads submerged. Those unaffected bent to,
tarring up blowy joins,

greasing refitted outboards, picking
stone from stone, or replaced in the mended day timber slips
time could eat. Holiday

cabins in rows now, someone's Christ
on cheap veneer, cod stink gone, Nescafé tin, cellophane bay
heaves, settles, but won't

uncrinkle as crab husks wash up
from the converted fish plant, crowns, their gulls attendant —
Biography's digital file,

adjusted, piles them totemic, ceramic,
serrated shins, and snaps No; meaning what could I know of it? Place,
position, effect, raised

a hic in tepid UC milk and water
I talk still like I'm from nowhere, or Ontario, and flood my head
with pretension having

lapsed since, if that's sayable, like
falling off porch steps into a hedge. Secular self grown peninsulaic,
won't budge, tides and

unlike elements squeezed in on three
sides but a view of the distant horizon held steady for decades;
cardiograph, whetstone, fine

thread to lean toward while attached,
mollusc, to a cold central mass. Consider both, do neither. Door key
fob is driftwood. Unleavened

pillow. Getaway rental ticks over
on lawn as near the storm door as held counsel is to the vatic register.
Word is belief. Check out's eleven.

Bathynaut

Plumb-bobbing gradations of lightlessness,
    super-pressurized other-
        worlds of Antarctic
coldcurrent and silence. Gauge needles
sweat, dither. It's all clown fish

at x leagues, near-nerveless bioluminescent
    tubes, their eyes on stalks,
        jaws afflicted with
cartoonish mandibular gigantism.
Bladders of bluey glow

without skeletons exo- or otherwise. Worms,
    freak-shrimp, splayed fans,
        phantom windsocks drift
crabwise in the black distance or move
millimetricly through clouds

of decomposing whale particulate, pesticidal
    weather systems spiralling
        through the hadal
depths irradiated as Litvinenko in a London
bed of whites pinning

blame where it belongs. Out the one lit portal,
    visible radius of mere metres,
        beyond which shadows
of colossal squid weave through quilts of coal
pitch shepherding their young

away to read in the coral forest, radiant heat
    of the magma kettle's geysering
        mineral font. And
mercury of industrial off-shot sieved
10,000 metres into pink

anemone, sightless puffers, sponge-cluster
    scrubbing grouted tiles of
        the Mariana Trench.
We'll ascend slowly. Up into Wood's Hole,
slowly. Quiet viewing room where

Alvin squats, dusted and somnolent, finished
    fetishizing the blood-bubble
        of depth. Windexed
to a gleam, roped off, what we'd expect
of a shelved head, outer

shell clam-enameled and connective hoses
    leading off to feigned
        air sources, audio contact.
Little exploratory pod, Little Boy's other
life. Guards dab at blistering

paint as and where museum light degrades it.

Industry
Song for Lutz Seiler

Thuringian boy sniper high in the guard tower, guy-wires
        bellying, no eastern wind.
The pastoral view said to roll and does, past stagnant acreage
        down to a river hectored
by hooded crows, bands of lawless swallows. The fields
        drag grit-cloud from Erfurt,
ragweed marches through fence line, on into low scrub
        where badgers pile shit that
dries slowly, spores settle in dust, a white moth waits
        for a white moon. Tailings
and milkweed, total weather, tea from a tin thermos. Radon

gas and new seepage. Ronneburg's cones. Waste rock moling
        out of the overburden exhaling
black dust, windborne isotopes. Heap leaching and In Situ
        Leaching. The Culmitzsch and
Trünzig ponds — azure moth, Wedgwood moth — like our Key
        Lake and Church Rock, lamps
of memory and infection, plume dispersion, history, and dam
        failure. How many klicks of the

Great Experiment's rail bed constructed of ticking composite,
        the systole and diastole of
molybdenum, vanadium, selenium, lead trucked north to
        Rostock, east into Russia. Central

planning or ill-luck that your childhood sat on uranium ore?
Could as easily have been pistols,
wristwatches, optical lenses, or mustard for the wurst trade.
Rights abuses in the extractive
sector. Free now, open pit. What is one voice but a resource?

Radio Tower

The pastoral dusted with icing sugar. Middle

Ontario in milky water. Madoc afloat.

Twilight. Everything's the colour of rabbits, scissored

from another world and pasted on thin, the eye not

distinguishing over there from way over there. Hour

of Eternal Return, applying base coats, patting front

pockets for keys. Cranberries, alembics, wheel

alignment. Mouths forming words but sentences

mock cricket song, holding out for full dark. Why plot

the Scenic Route if we're just going to point to blight

and obsolete tillers? Back home wall mirrors

wait like pie crusts for the boiled fruit of us.

Partly to do with half-hearing weak signals fade.

Five minutes to the hour — We're still taking calls —

Late-day cradled in wobbling aspic. Semi-rural glazed

doe. Kanata Wave Pool waves to a Hercules circling Trenton.

Brief Coherence

Strange on a common Tuesday to slide into wakefulness
  sensing contentment as a soft charge
in the room's air, as if reaching from below covers
  might prove sufficient to all the burnt

years stripping the self of encumbrance. It hovers just
  above the bed's heat. *Will we be equal*
to the day? — translated into less stringent terms,
  taking on the gentler yellows of pleasure. Before

vision, or the limbs' jointed timber shifts, language forges
  agreement with at least one built seam
of the world: "VIA Rail now has wi-fi on the Windsor-Quebec
  corridor." I peg into my jeans at peace.

Tire water's bonnet of gnat cloud. Splintered pallets, grass
  groomed by snow-press. Raft from scrap ply,
tar-paper, and bones of a doghouse. Brief coherence. Spring
  floods. Our neighbour then, a Mrs. Westlake,

would taxi her long cigarettes, peasant tunics, elaborate
  manicures and lips across conjoined
lawns on afternoons in summer to visit with Mum, and
  I'd sprawl on the tight-weave nylon carpet

face down exposing my little boy's back to her glue-ons.
  Knife-spiders. Spine conductors. Partly
eavesdropping on adults, but this new trouble, stiffened
  gauge calibrated to the earth's core. Such gothic

tangles of old oak, leeches, beagles, and drought. Muskrats
   nailed to limbless trunks. Threat of tetanus.
But Tuesday's unveiling, languid, and like Liverpool
   I'm unrecognizable on the road, fearless, fluid,

spread to the lines, creating more than occupying space,
   foreign-owned but adhering to the hymn,
You'll Never Walk Alone, though who's accompanying who
   still grates. Hydraulic scorpion pulverizing

the sidewalk. Old lead pipes, lake water. Percussion and
   blinking orange hazard lights. Having hacked
the euonymus back to bare wood, living sinks to rhythm
   and work. Magnolia candling near men in X'd vests.

Wesleyan Kettle

Pneumatic-looking sprung tube
apparatus holding the door open. Serious heat.

Purpling capelin
being processed in the tub.

"My name's _____ and dis ears me brudder
Shan. We lives in de same ouse."

Butane extracted
from filched Bics.

Car seat on springs
pulled up to a pit.

Quaker Oats. Cigarettes, teaberry, Jordache —

By dusk they lashed
each other with rods and hooks.
At speed, the tackle whistled.
I left as a shimmering spinner
set in Shawn's neck like a tic.
The tamarack stilled.

Impetigo.

Salt solution in a wash basin.
White basin, white breakers.

Ontario plates.
She'd swab clogs of moistened
cereal from nostrils, mouth
and neck.

Whatever it meant, it lodged.
I went and sought them out.

Hunter Deary and Hospital Wing

Hunter Deary emits noises like peach pits;
  dry, scrotal humming that punctuates fits.
When a hip comes loose it comes loose
  before breakfast and she pops it back in

with a winch, a rock, a clean tube and hemp belt.
  Ask Hunter Deary what the microbes
are for. Ask Hunter Deary what the library's
  for. Ask Hunter Deary what agent con-

tested her birthright, her staying out late, her
  transmission on broadband at night.
The men in the neon X. The hole in the
  plastic. The ppb. The stitches. The snug.

The snug. The stitches. The parts per billion.
    Hospital Wing sings to his children.
Children of blood lung.
Children of static.
    Hospital Wing sings to his children.
The snug. The stitches. The parts per billion.

Hunter Deary has clicked on the task pane
  reads there what they cut from the thought:
a topographical map of the region, a vein
  darkening wetlands, strung north through

some temperate zone. Hunter Deary left gas
  in a bird's nest, bags under bypasses,
phenobarbital in the mud of the Don. Hunter
  Deary in traction. Hunter Deary in Huntsville.

She's counting down days to a hearing, fed on
  black pumpkin, on cheese string, on
marrow sucked through wing of an auk. Ages
  in ice bubble. Calving. The fake vermillion.

Calving. Ice bubbles. The fake vermillion.
  Hospital Wing sings to his children.
Children born sexless and cleansed.
Leaded gametes in frog ponds.
  Hospital Wing sings to his children.
Calving. The ages. The fake vermillion.

Coney Burns

While simmering through two
less a day first in Mimico,
then Kingston, for theft
over a grand,
assault and
possession,
Burns found a pen pal
in the late-period Auden
who'd himself recently
lost Kallman
and was considering
proposing
to Hannah Arendt
happily married
in her rent-controlled
upper east side
walk up.
Coney'd been privately
stewing since the fiasco
in Orangeville
over notions of justice,
love, the despair
unto death, and theories
of structural
disequilibrium,
so uncorked all he'd bottled
into wandering,
spectral, ill-spelled
letters composed
near the stainless

steel en suite
bowl he was made nightly to
scrub after reading
his Böll, Bowles,
Bellow, his Bello'cq,
far beneath the pitted
orb burning bone-
white over the exercise
yard, second-hand milk
sieved through his
window's grillwork
and known
in its Italian form
to Leopardi, Negri,
Ovid, in a way,
and increasing numbers
of Romany:

...and stooped over
my day shifts pushing
the wheely bins of soiled
bedding I've thought
of that Belgian, Alÿs,
pushing his block
of white ice through
Mexico City's bleached
streets, his Chuck
Taylors' rubbery
ankle crests blooming
penumbras of damp.
By mission's end
in the video

three boys are seen
looking up from prodding
the weird clear remnant
pooling there on the Avenida;
some lens grinder's
mistake in the lake
of its own disappearance,
or the first instance of
an invasive
jellyfish species
made landfall from the
lung shadow of the Gulf's dead
zone. They look up, across
the unbridgeable chasm
that keeps three — no, two,
now — worlds in their
respective spheres
and flash hand-signs
for victory or peace.
Then they show us
their teeth. I mention
all this in the spirit
of "shit that occurs to me"
but also of course as
response or addendum
to comments you generously
shared in your last
on Xtian theology's
endgame in your
view as the only transcendent,
accessible levelling
force. There's this, too:
one oncoming Wednesday

in June, a Cree
kid near Gypsumville
will lift his face
from a dense
bouquet of gasoline
to meet the incoming
darts of a taser
gun. Picture trained deerflies
rigged to forked lightning.
He bursts into flame.
Third-degree
over two-thirds of
his body. We're free, I'm afraid,
to frame this to mean
any number of things, each
truth a shade
poorer than its progenitor.
I saw a bay finch
on the big fence shiver,
earlier, before starting
this letter.

To Inflame the Civic Temper
— William James

Hey, Assface in the Hydroplane!
Nut-vice in the Prius!
Headcheese on the Snowmobile!

Dick in the Pontoon Boat!
Handjob in the Humvee!
PervSquirt on the Custom Ducati!

Smacked Ass in the Harvester!
Nipple Pincher in the El Camino!
Cock Wipe in the Recycling Truck!

Motherfucker in the Radio Flyer!
Skank in the Bathysphere!
Crotch Rot in the Big Rig!

Douche Face on the Rattling Dray!
Moron on your Ten Speed!
Shit Monkey in a Swamp Boat!

Ratfuck in your Moonboots!
Monkeytard in the Crab Boat!
Cumlicker in the Dirigible!

Goat's bag in the Highway Grader!
Ass rash on the gorgeous Vespa!
Hey, Toilet Raider on the LRT!

Chicken Rapist in the Sailboat!
Stall Creeper in the Helicopter!
Ahoy there! Ahoy!

I said, Ahoy!!

Fending Off the Conservatism in Adorno

At the festering corner of Boston and Queen
The Tasty Chicken House clings through May to its Christmas
tinsel, and is not long for this world.
Sanctioned colour murals under bubble script tags
won't slow the winds of progress. Next door,
Wattle and Daub, a law firm of Newfoundlanders
or a crafts supply in keeping with the poultry theme,
smells weakness, softens its smuggest aspects
with miniature jingle bell over the gripey hinge.
Knot your scarf … *comme ça*. The Speech Pathologist,
just blocks from here, requests we enter through
the rear. Uck, ook, echk, esh, eesch, ess. Mushy dentates,
audibly aspirant at the front end, he's describing
the texture of the tuscan soup I made. Wading into names
he'll enter the depletion that refuses names.
Lower on Logan, near Eastern, the Weston plant
rolls out its bread trucks well past dawn. Rousseau
had that bit about brioche in his *Confessions* a year prior
to Marie Antoinette's arrival in France. Luxury
bread's now a four-pound cow pat of walnut sourdough
that petrifies by Wednesday. What class are we?
When did we last love music and not its function
as calmative or its causativity? He gets down.
Leather strop, lengths of chain. The white sky a light box
viewed as gaps between negatives of the inverted city,
bike lock, bike lock, first bank in Regent Park,
the auratic properties of this chapstick tube, and
damp stringy tree-hair peeled from the inner bark.
Guy Ben-Ner, from his tree house, said,
"in *Wild Boy*, for example, my son really does utter

his first English word on-screen. He gets his first
haircut and you see" — I'll never fully — "you see
him barely managing to dress alone
for the first time." What we mistake for popular song
blows out its hair near the window-mounted
air-con unit. Wet snare drum in the patronymic,
imagine seeing what's there. A turtle — softer meats
within a patterned armour — might be its patterned armour.

Que Syria, Syria

Slide whistle and shit bucket. We'll do
our own rendition. Convictions, like haircuts,
hold true until the morning they don't.
I'll be proved wrong down the road —
not far down the road, mind you;
likely just past the next gum coin,
before that streetlight retrofitted
to look more *lampish*. Why are disarticulated
feet washing ashore in their Nike carapaces
like hermit crabs adjusting to habitat loss?
The North Pacific Gyre spits out basketballs,
pen caps, rat-tail combs for the well-behaved
and habitually cagey. Kids, eh? I could have
taken prisoners but lack administrative skills,
all those numbers followed by letters followed
by answering to Amnesty and ghosts
bringing in ghosts that exit as corpses.
I have my suspicions. It's just I doubt their validity.
I take my legs off above the knee, lean
both against the armoire, and slide into Chopin
while tomorrow balls up its tinfoil and begins to chew.

To When We No Longer Die

We have all we don't want now and can't
know need, though the Victorian terminal's still
visible from here. Its shell freshly sand-blasted,

and what iron still veins those windows
gives them a lumpen aspect, like trowelled-on
mud in the winter of an era deeply previous to —

unnamed calendrical marker fading fast
into movie wars, pundits in seizure, and fragments
from Lincoln's speeches. Latin U's appear as V's,

we can't help wondering were they missing
a particular chisel blade. Rock doves
decorate the gothic cake in cack. Shot

in black and white, we're to choose colour
tone and contrast later, in post-production,
once we're past the very teenage tristesse

of imagining ourselves gone, all art-house taciturn,
crises of finitude, and very little make-up. Ranks
of the *as it was ever it shall be*, still smoking. Treble clefs

of black squirrels, meanwhile, change to bass as a wind
gets up in the far-off branch work. We'd like
to be remembered for not mucking

up the place. Are songs litter? Is there an alley
we have yet to piss in? Accelerating heads whip past
in illuminated diorama, flip-book depicting

the one head. Our own train slows. We re-take
our seats in separate compartments, tot up
turkey vultures, imports from Arkansas, glaring

at congested cloverleafs. Mid-range drone of turbines
above sugar beets and alpaca. Appearance proclaims
itself the original mystery. Northern life migrates north.

Sparklehorse

He's upright.
We'll take that
as a good sign.

But the quivering
lip, the pillars

of blue light,
the wind machine?

Honey, I need to sit —

These? These are scorch-
marks in the
Varathane.

Russian Doctor
for David Foster Wallace

I.

There's what's envisioned and there's what
      arrives. I was overheating
in the sun reading Chekhov's "Lady With a Dog,"
      de-bubbled coffee foam crusting

to a blanched scum, a wasp trading recon
      flights with two sparrows
over the rubble of oat muffin. I was content,
      or not buying what the shops

were selling; either way, when the young girl
      with her mum and her cocoa
asked for a puppy I was overhearing her life
      lifting off from the adjacent

table. I could smell her hair; a plastic butterfly
      clip pinning black bangs back.
Watermelon. Cotton. The next time she spoke
      it would destroy me. So I paused,

glancing up over my own shoulder, where I normally
      position the author, and an agitated,
sculptural woman with Modernist hair
      addressed me, "I need a paper!

I need to know if I'm still in first place!" Her
		mouth had that distinctive
motional autonomy as though someone behind
		her spoke through a hole

cut out of her face. Yanked up from inside
		enjoyment, damaged perception
builds masks for the real. Mentally, I wiffled through
		hockey pool, bridge scores, obituaries,

and plain bat shit before asking the obvious —
		"A fishing derby here on the lake,
I caught a fish." A big fish I'm guessing —
		She shifted, her head occluded

the sun and it was suddenly like being in Chicago
		submitting to a Mies van der Rohe from
down in the engineered gulch. I closed one eye to
		the silhouette. "If it stands I win thirty

grand and get entered in the fish-off on Friday."
		"Excuse me?" It was the mouth/face
disjunct. "One-day fish-off for one million bucks!"
		She cupped her own elbows as though

nursing an angler's cramp. I pictured three fingers
		hooked through the flared gills
of what she told me were stocks of Chinook. Her wedding
		band glinted. I went back to my book

hoping the problem of being with others might
    resolve itself gently while the fan
in the air duct whirred, twinned worlds — the one between
    pages and this one with a face — collided,

merged, story stitched us into the summer like ants
    marking a line through our spills.
Long days like armchairs we leave our impressions
    in, loving the possible landscape.

2.

The worst of the glare slid behind the sales lot tinsel
    and she wasn't a stranger at all. No
stranger; my neighbour, Liz. Elizabeth Abbott.
    You may know her work: *Celibacy*,

Mistresses, something on Haiti, and recently, *Sugar*.
    Her home a hospice for dying dachshunds,
way station for incoming rescues from Serbia (we nearly
    took in Dunja last month). So, animal

rights activist, retired academic, vegan, but here's where
    the Danish gets sticky. Just last week it dawned
on me, in a dinghy adrift on Georgian Bay, while rethinking
    the preponderance of pumpkins in *The Life*

and Times of Michael K, while the sun crested the horizon
    over Huron and settled like a South African
in Brisbane, before I'd had either coffee or chance to tally
    the consequences, it came to me, Coetzee — J. M., *him* —

had modeled *Elizabeth Costello* on this Elizabeth Abbott.
    I know what you're thinking, but stop. I looked
them up. A conference, Belgrade, '91, they shared
    keynote address three ways with Martha Nussbaum

and must have had, at the very least, lunch, if not more.
    I know what you're thinking. *He'*d submitted
a paper but was, shocker, turned down: "Paranoia: Can We
    Live Among the Animals?" —R. Karadzic.

Can this be about faces? Not forced concordances, farce,
    or puppetry. Assemblies of holes, nerves, ligature,
and skin leading creaturely selves through time.
    Coins, stamps, like confetti from the wedding

of heaven and hell, food riots and this view, where
    the ailanthus sheds bits seasonally, a tanager
tears through morning, and the air writhes, ionized,
    saturated, a new face in contour where no face was.

3.

"There were three compulsory hand-
      washing stations,
poster boards with clear diagrams
      of correct method
and duration, and just beyond that
      you were fitted with
a protective mask, those crisp, papery,
      white mouth-aprons
that loop your own breath back into
      your nose." My wife

had splayed the Chekhov face down
      on her chest, her calm, her
recall seemed blown down from the ceiling
      fan, a weird tenor inhered
in her speech, so I listened without
      looking. "Two shrinks
in lab whites I found unnerving
      enough, but worse, they insisted
we proceed with our talk in spite
      of the masks. I'd begun

imagining neither one had a mouth.
      Their contributions, such
as they were, sounded autovocally
      croaked through the creased
folds of their respiratory prophylactics."
      I was unsure why my wife
was talking like this. "And so
      anemically lit, like a chapel
or throat. I remember feeling depleted,
      tired. I'd never again speak

as honestly of my past as I was speaking
then with that orchid fastened
over the lower half of my face. Orchid?
The fibrous, disposable
half-shell afloat on the still reservoir
pooling between those
two doctors and I." Powerful image, I
offered. "Of what? Please, tell me."

A watermelon section rocked untouched
on the bedside table,
black seeds scattershot in the paling red.
Something had snapped.
A connective thread, tensile, elastic, now
withdrawing or receding
back to its pre-contact shape. It addressed
our room with the damp
seething hiss of a bivalve shucked
from its root-stump.

4.

Parquet in herringbone stuck between channels

shadow of the long leash and paint

on grass blades marking the water main

Spent D-batteries girdled in white tape

Torn moon ferried on a gurney over clay shingle

and the crawl of wing lights

Scalloped fencing

the plane trees in rows, a child meets

the aggregrate gravel down on his knees

The lavender looked putrid and the air stank

It was my machinery ruined

what France grew

so I lay down in my kitchen to go

I Think I Will Go to Bakersfield

Having Ellesmere'd the hardwood with dropsheets
I pulled what I could from the telescoping handle,
plunged the new roller into
East Texas Fence Line as
a cabbage moth Gramsci'd around
the cage light
then

<<<<-ed

and

>>>>-ed

gently a bit to milk off the excess.
My intention was to paint my perception
of the paint in paint while extending an open palm
to the viewer who'd later come
with bedroll and abscess
to use the room.
What can I say,
I'm done.

Gives You Cuddles?

Robert Rauschenberg 1925–2008

I forget where I was when Podborski caught an edge

and I gleaned a little of the two-way bleed betwixt courage

and folly. *Twix*: the first bite's like the starter's gate at Kitzbühel,

you can see the upper rim of the "Mouse fall"

then nothing. Bronze foil, descent into pure white, wood

past the crash fence. It could

be the same everywhere. The obit, back of the sports page,

says your Cherokee mother [sic] once made a skirt

from the back panel of the dark suit

her brother lay buried in. Silent cage,

I scrape the cedar shavings, the cooled dung.

Our urge

to know the particular life — fit deprivation into its slot as The Age

assembling itself from facts on the ground — paces

up for a closer gawk at the paint, the pieces,

glue-ons, rub-offs, erasures,

globbing up our access to, our acceptance of change.

Bricolage,

the birth pangs of equanimity under an onslaught of garbage.

Discussing image, tone, candour, judge-

ment, and the like, I said, "Less sobbing bird,

more burnt ox." And that afternoon overheard

a deckhand off Juno reformulate truth, "Every hour spent

de-icing is an hour spent

not crabbing." Proximity. Glue. Two or more streams merge,

we get a place name in Huron or Cree. Fabergé

egg, crushed Fanta can. Before Captiva —

Maker, Milton — you did Dante

good. Thought box thrown in the river

Styx. Cradle cap. Plover.

Hologram, Aubade

A.M. Axe or adze? Blame the tang on Stelco.
A crow's shadow shoots
the full length of the black locust —
down, then right back up it again.
The dew already burnt off the carrots.
Dog's nose, or detonator tip
of an upturned shuttlecock like
something silo'd under the mown lawn.

Original Thingist, remember Texas?
Jackrabbits mimicking oil derricks, to less
effect, though they suffered the earth's shudders.
I just make it up —

cheap Cuervo, flea flickers in shopfront chapels, and
the tumoured bench seat of a Rambler with a history.

What if it's all meant to work
the way it's fashioned now, no
other binding property or force?

In the coming work stoppage, front-end
loaders will dragon off
to pick their teeth barracked in the municipal
pit. There's a food cache near
the tire swing. Crow knows you
know it knows you know.

When the prop shark died its tooth
became first talisman then decorative
then forensically interesting
in a two-part episode of *Hoarders*.

World-view of a killhorse, loosehorse,
not that you ever saw it coming
but you saw a Cassandra coming.

Quarter mile from the Polish men's choir
of frogs near a culvert, their kekking and blanging
bewilderment's agent on earth. Night's idiot
vestments now piled in the gorge. What
an accomplishment, the scarred softball!
Stand inside the dome
of sumac — what, phantom, do you feel?

Sobjectivist

You stepped out of a network of interrelations,
    no, you stepped into a sterilized clearing,
        a pause in the general
    havoc, and remembered what the deadly

snake had said: *What am I for, if not to bury*
    in the mud? What am I for,
        if not to die? A galactic wind
    reared up and a whistle rode in its saddle

as if someone not far from where you hovered
    expressed contentedness,
        an ease in themselves
    normally found only in the lower-order life

forms, tortoises under their deco domes, herbivorous
    prairie dogs, drooling cod,
        Kelly green tree
    frogs, and the beneficial nematodes. Hailing

the traveller, you've fogged up the visor, so suddenly
    it's like looking through tears
        to a spot in the middle
    distance where you'd much rather be. Must

we always be losing heat? What about landmarks?
    There was a knoll a ways back,
        an atoll off to the east
    blackened by ash and long denuded of native

flora. The snake had a point; in fact, he had many, and
    they constituted a line segment
        shooting off at a vector.
    We can calculate X by drifting off to sleep,

as if sleep were a set of coordinates indicating plains
    of open ocean. It's hard to concentrate
        juice in the rain.
    No sooner had the whistling lowered to a moan

when out of Nowhere appeared a Place. *What time
    is it?* It's late. *Who said that?*
        I am the snake. It's very
    late, and you don't know where your people are.

A Pharaoh in Moosonee

ONR's *Polar Bear Express* out of Cochrane

brattling over a high trestle, feeders to the Moose River
a brown cocktailed from snake oil and stubby,
motor oil and cola. Fir
and jack pine of the hardening
drift out into Siberian distance.
O biggest biome trekking poleward.
Orange vinyl bib

on the headrest. Then, a boat.
Isn't there always a boat. Diminished,
Conradian remnants with bird glasses
spitting into the mining runoff. Low sun, September,
the white-wash on the deck rail a visual analogue
to chewing breath mints. We'd lucked
into the blindered good sense to limit
the surreptitious pics to Cincinnati divorcées spilling
out of leopard print, tawny super-curls awhip
in the subarctic wind.

Gas and water in aboveground pipeline
goring the town's gravelled middle, seeping
at the bolted joins, shade
for the sphagnum, foil, and northern stitchwort.

Massive, choked-looking ravens,
bullish breath plumes from
the nail holes in their carbon-graphite, ichthyosauran beaks,
rake-footed, they gobble rocks, check
for pit sweat.

Newly armed with a new slingshot (a *slingshot*) —
its phlegm-coloured surgical hose — I
wouldn't take your hand
where the teepee flung its skirts back over struts
and whale-ribbing, guy-wires chewing grooves
into a ground stake. Tapering, feline ink lines,
cadmium infill on a beluga's
foreshortened, babyish fore-skull.
Nylon K-way collapses into its pouch,
afternoon heats up, a field kettle, bannock on a rock beach
they called Fossil Island. Imagine.

The Evinrude on the big canoe.

Sign after sign from Moose Factory south to Tecumseh —

Nottawasaga

Sky a motif of cowslip in clear ice,

mayflies make moon-dials of the flagstones.

One hawk. Second hawk. They were up there

earlier, as sand toads tacked from grass tuft to grass

tuft, up the pressed dune's incline. Divots

under the pin oak.

Lake level's low. Unlike

This American Life's female executive producer's testosterone ...

E. coli trucked in

on lettuce, bocce lessons, pine beetle.

The shooter games vibrate in Balm Beach

Arcade so we squint, the better to look the part

and later leak over *The Guardian*. Re-apply after bathing.

Contrail or cloud pattern? We're late arrivals, like winter.

One week, cedar fence to the waterline. Next,

a passion play of flip flops. Husqvarna. An arm splint.

Hoping Your Machine Can Handle the Big Image

Look, at an indeterminate juncture
        of my sixth year, I was moved to wed my purpose
to the graphic depiction of man

combing sense out from the knotted tangle of necessity

with event. 4H, or Jader Seed, or the Rotary
        Club had sponsored a poster campaign, on the theme
of farm safety, and I'd been inclined to think

of myself as *above the herd* when it came to one dozen

Crayola, arrangement of interpretive glyphs,
        primitivist use of prime colour, perspective, and
the slightly flattened, lowercase "m"s flocking

persistently up- and outward to a sheet's NNE

corner. I'd never, up to then, short of church-sponsored
        hay rides, been on a farm, or smelled the horneted,
chaffy old leather and striped light of a proper loft.

But how I ached to effect public opinion. I was earth

newly turned, baking in the heat of emergency;
        the very *un-safe*ness of harvest, the daily and flagrant
peril those agrarian classes toiled within shone into

my heart, drafting there an idea of justice in burnt sienna —

Initial concepts smouldered in the pitfire of the obvious:
      pitchforks were sharp, like needles, leaning
against barn walls, godless tridents, their eye-skewers

arced neglectfully outward. Flame and hay were like hay

and flame. Dung's greased, hazardous lubricant appeared
      underfoot pell-mell in pre-dawn's unpasteurized light.
It all either wouldn't boil down to pictorial shorthand,

or played like a back-forty Hanna-Barbera. I drew a hole.

A mare's ankle, twin toddlers, and five hogs disappeared
      like heat into the hole's black wax. I liked working
in gummy, spidered dust near the chewed and louvred

edges of wooden stair runners. Cereals, salted nuts, cinched

in a faux-naugahyde marble pouch. Crosscut, two inches
      thick, of hardwood, crenellations of bark stained red,
chapter and verse seared into its topographical map.

(Outside, Parmalat and Collier Grain turning the vise on small-
holdings by indirect means, Chicago tickertaped and bloating.)

Dreaming others' dreams of inheritance and succession

I filled the background with harvest wheat, pulled the blue
      wash down to meet its tips, then drafted a combine
in profile, forest green, mastodon mowing arable land stalled

in cut stubble to spit from its spreader chute one

arm entire. Detached, serrated, pointing Cistinely at
       its drained farmer, stood lidless in the bib of shadow
his cap's beak cast. Stunned, regretful, disproportionate.

Arterial leak of time in vermillion. Barn cats behind the silo

silo in front of the sun. Though I knew enough to make
       of his mouth a truncated line segment, the design
placed second behind a predictable gas leak and fireball.

Perspective means objects capitulate, finally, under
       prolonged grievance, to a visual rightness. I used
a straight-edge on each hexagonal lug-nut.

Ledger

I lived, then, above a neglected corner store. Milk
    was cheap. Converted cinema, its storage
room staged the seasonal influx of fruit fly, the floor
    sloped down to the dairy and meat fridge.

I'd reduced my furnishings, since being left to fend
    there, to lamp stands, bookcase, table
and CD player. Configuring the small emptied
    talismans of my own loneliness

so they stared back, hoping they'd inscribe
    an identity onto what was left
after chewing away at the core for a decade.
    The sour cotton-batting-and-vinyl

trauma of irreducible young man's narcissism.
    Such drama. I'd become evening,
the illogic and armour of liquor. Likely nothing
    I did in those years could be called

good in the ledger, if one exists, but once, past
    midnight, below where I soaked in
Kid A's anhedonic bath under a bald light,
    on the corner of Galley and Roncesvalles

Avenue, a woman stood pressing her kids' heads
    to her hip as if waiting for glue to dry,
her bloated luggage stonehenged on my verge
    of charred lawn, still tagged for Pearson.

And though my window was not television, threat
        appeared, predictably, as a Dodge Charger
with matte primer. It had circled twice, and on
        this third pass all of her flinched, she pulled

the kids close, quailing back from the curb. Whoever
        drove taunting her now — proposition
or insult — so she was mouthing no and scanning
        the blank streets and turning one

shoulder as not to antagonize. It can't be oversold,
        the human capacity to form alliance,
however fragile or contingent, through a hornets'
        swarm of gesticulation and masks

of non-aggression. To traverse or bypass language
        proper — Spanish-speaking, she'd
arrived, I learned later, from San Salvador — and make
        clear somehow that a small arena

of relative safety had opened. She brought the children
        inside. To the landing halfway up
the stairs and asked for a telephone. The toddler
        picked at paint bubbling on the baseboards —

it takes so long to really arrive. Their minor city
        of luggage, wrapped in clear plastic
like some mariner's kit or evidence of quarantine,
        I lugged under the awning. We didn't

touch. We were a family, and I would soon learn
      the names of my children. I got them
juice, and looked a long while at a dishtowel. Printed
      montage of vacant stone mills, treed

glens, clock towers and ridiculous sheep. The CD
      stuck on that aerated gurgle and rev
between tracks. At some point they left. At
      some point they all must have left.

Merganser and Minnow

*

Boys after bath and *S.W.A.T.* repeats
flung under
bedsheets, pen lights
and Solid State portables
set between Buffalo
and the fuzz of bafflement —

in the mooned tent,
night light's weak soup,
submerged, muffled syllable,
Carter into Ray-gun, Tehran
becoming Navarone.

It's 3 ft deep or so so
they go in groups, skimming their
ribbed basin floor. They go
and feed in groups

*

Jacquard loom's little card.
"Lake" in teletype, spilled chad box
and the punched tape.
Piano roll in the shallows.
Fortran in full sun doing
fluid dynamics.

Lesson in epiphenomenal
hyphenation —
it arises from but is
not of.

Hand nets dragged, bowed,
you needed a pail — was it? —
with perforated base
to severalize nouns from their shadows.

Sovereign

Hospital lobby staging a jumble sale, so being discharged's
    like viewing San Marco. The Habs in deep
down in Philly, Ballack has sent Liverpool home.
    Light of midday like chlorine after the postnatal

dim, those Danby mums on hardboard dulled down
    the ward. His Baba and Dedo took him
home in the Honda. Hollowed out. Air strains clean through;
    I'm a canoe. Ghost-nippled, rose-petalled,

cross-eyed narcoleptic — *No power higher than myself save*
    what I ceded to the State at birth. Sweet William!
Not my son, blooms trimming the parking garage, bruised
    strip of the vast conurbation, they nice up

the joint, along with the mayor. Aced the Apgar. Not an
    improper moment, is it, to think the city might
as yet work, bear out *Solvitur Ambulando* at street
    level while no one's looking. That journalist,

held in Gaza in a locked room, aghast at travellers'
    impatience the day he's released, six
short weeks later stood carping at the absence of buses
    in London. Pillow cloud, cinnamon roll,

health card, I feel ... *altered.* We change, and change back
    as though adaptation were Cuba. Walking
traffic down the sunless canyon of Grenville, why wouldn't
    you open your face to me, here? Am I not

the sun, lugging these birthing bags and cut flowers and
       charged with keeping a lid on explosions
into futurity into what's next? When will the bricks speak?
       Passing the raised gate of the pay-parking

an Escalade pulls out and the banded arm drops, candy
       cane guillotine, to clean the overheated mind.
Knocked out. Knocked into the engine oil and cellophane.
       Knocked back toward *techne*, to-do lists,

today's handlot of small majesties with mass, surface, scent.

Brno

In a low-beamed, medieval garret
over the Czech Experimental Theatre

his better v-neck sweater
had begun to unravel,

as he'd unravelled, begun to parrot
inanities at the ghost of Václav Havel —

"ghost" as Havel'd
been and gone two nights prior —

from the hand-tooled church pews
of the theatre bar. Sternest vows,

firm opinions, seeded in the abyssal gulch
between Pembroke, Arnprior,

Smith's Falls
and Renfrew's

sadder fringes, revealed themselves
as re-circulated views filched

from higher journals, contingent
on travel, circumstance, mood, expedience.

Dormer window framing the Basilica's Q-tips.
Let's look in: a columnar light

that isn't his light
streams through, pools at the chair legs, his fingertips

crab and hook at the new SIM
card and Vodafone PIN.

He won't reach home.
He'll conjure, then annihilate it, then he'll go numb.

As in the passport photo, his smile's slapped off,
the background's bled white,

and when he looks up
he's looking up

into the end of *Catastrophe.*
Which they say is a study

on the violence of direction
but could as well be the direction

violence took
when freed from the jaws of The Book.

Weren't all nihilists
great believers first?

The bigger they come, etc.
I came big, contained multitudes, etc.

He thinks of his son:
how before he turned one

he knew how to sit,
how to sit and brood.

As Lowell on the Ringbahn

Lowering sinker and lure in the Spree,
I like to imagine Albert E. lecturing at Humboldt,
                    I bet he never wept.
Scything the new, chilled air over Moabit —
skeletal, balletic — the cranes insist
                    we graph it out
from up in the EU yellow and blue. Cost
of jet fuel per person, cost of Khartoum.
                    Egypt at the Pergamon. Jeffs
at the Hamburger Bahnhof, again,
Koons and Wall, or always, and the man
                    in Mauerpark market
raking crop circles in crêpe batter
over a heated skillet.
                    Wherever one sleeps, here,
train rails converge near enough
to make of dreams a dentist's chair.
                    Benign, punctual
whine as Systems
Theorists stare into tram cables webbing
the cutaway,
Prenzlauer Berg's advancing pram fleet,
                    Zoo attendance vs
bull elephant's heart rate —

They knew I was "American" by
               the uninhibited use
made of the flat's windows. Panoptically
               giving on to the neighbours'
flats across a central courtyard, I looked into
the neighbours' flats, across the central courtyard,
               and having seen enough of eros
and despair, took down from Saeed's
vast shelf DeLillo's *Americana*:

The true
audience is darkness itself. We unwrap
our lives to it, trying to appease the monkey
What monkey? I said
The Viennese monkey.

               Blue-faced ducks
weirdly upright like dodos in the shadow
               of the Russian Embassy.
Young men with tall cans dangle
from the riveted loops. They sing
               as they sway, then go.
Centre circumnavigated in less than an hour,
               seen through a living puzzle
of rain. Tiergarten throbbing alder, old oak, black pond.

The End of Air Travel

Hand-crank your shortwave, recline.
Juncos return after the cold snap.

No more parallel pin lights
on the aisle carpet transecting

great circles off Greenland.
No more hard butter.

You won't see their summer
place on the Cornwall coast,

or recognize your duffle
by its bulge, coughed like a lozenge

onto the segmented belt.
Remember how customs felt?

You're full of metal
but being full of metal

is now a question for relatives,
lawyers, land area,

and OBGYNs, their Geiger
counters out-clicking the squirrels.

If we must walk to low-density sectors, so be it,
carrying kids in columns,

and columns of hazard flashes stunning the rosehip.
Blooms of regret over the mail-slot,

the free weeklies fanned over polyvinyl
in buckshot waiting rooms,

as upper echelons in underground bunkers
decode code. Bears in blue skips

model with sherbet tubs
what to do in the event of.

Skirt of milkweed under
new phone masts relaying

intentions to sleep or scream,
yawn or grin through the quiet interregnum.

Avalon, Helicopter

Morning desacralized, the quack
science of fog. Moisture condensing
around airborne granules of salt, it's *cloud*
when we make out the silhouette

of a duck. Spit, the air
hits supersaturation and spits back. Gulls beyond
the first veil: clown's horn lashed
to the handlebars with stiff wire —

Hermit thrush on the near fencepost, beaded
meniscus in the bleached syringe.
Electroshock, duster, blot. One crow's drawn-out ablutions.
If Berkeley, as we hope, misfigured the contents, and ideas

are like other things, here, on a porcelain toadstool
sprouted from powerlines, is the sum of all past assertions
on essence. Underfoot sponge,
mystery mounds, moss ottomans, and everyone's addition

shearing away from first additions. Wild rose,
tin well cap, purple iris in the juniper tangle where a brook
bogs out from up on the cape's moonscape.
Shrew and owl. Confectioners

table of black shale where the clapboard claps out.
Tut's lost prick a wasp drips out of.

Whoever it was ransacked the ossuary built
this hitching post doohicky for the clothesline's antipodal pulley.

Scalded wrack. What's the local term?
Sippy cup in the shed
near the chainsaw and widowed oar.
Breaking the Bakelite surface out there,

a minke bends into the first, the only,
race gate — two grebes —
of his zen GS. On day one
of the home fishery, Michael, over a platter
of cod, "The real is not mental,
it's *mental*" as the pup tent fwaps, lifts anchor.

Evening's a tranche of kids on bog bikes,
Big 8 Cola, the dew line, Sikorski bolts,
Purity Crackers, WikiLeaks, and sea smoke.

Futility Music

The shiny spot's decoy, sometimes
emotive, sometimes in bright digression
                         — Peter Gizzi

The Don Valley Parkway a stopped
drain mid-strike, July,

undergirded, holding the valley's
contours and sponging up light.

Fluttering lame-bats of petro-waste
garland the fashion district,

downtown core, isolated baize
that abuts the lake. Pink-and-milk snaggy

shreds on leisure boat masts,
maypoles if we can manage *ebullience*.

Not murmuring across the 49th, not aimed, I'm not —

northern black widow's young
disperse to garages farther north,

possums, giant hogweed, blistered kids
and robins in Inuktitut,

spores, strains, clustered blues
showing high

growth rates in formerly arid
Escarpment and Green Belt.

The BofC sets interest at an unbelievable
whatever, so ultimate Frisbee, so

terrace talk, renovations, maple suckers
wearing reflective foil

*

And why chili dogs in Jackson near the Pen?

What in Petawawa after Iowa with a foot-pedal and pot?

The point of Fort St. John? Hanlan's Point?

Why then Galway? Come By Chance? Tweed? Kispiox?

From whence came light to Ajax, Split, Rivière-du-Loup?

What in Harbour Grace? Passing through Hengelo to Itzehoe

What's Oslo? Liguria why? Why Genoa?

What went through Batoche? Bialystok? Ben Bulben?

Explain Moosonee, Moose Factory. Pusan in terms of Ulsan.

Ten lines on Sydney, Sydney Mines.

Kingston or Kingston or Bay Bulls or Eston or Euston?

What the Hull? Why must Now end Here?

*

You're treading the tailwaters,
beyond the eddy where it shallows

polishing mid-size riverstone
that knock, calypso in gentle

triplets and kick drum echo,
when your head dips and re-crests

seeing water spiders skulling
off the near bank and stalks of cress

or rushes bend oblique beneath cutline
but arrow up as per light's air

logic if you gator your eyes
over the meniscus and algal dusts.

Sun coined on rhubarb, the current
speaking Russian to ears cut in half.

Skeena's headwaters, the Stikine,
the Nass nickel-plated, nulled in rock gas,

blunt chorus I heard while lifting
the warped door gnawing the threshold

to boil cabbage, mop with a capful of vinegar.
If it's on its way, we should greet it.

Acknowledgements

Several of the poems appeared, often in earlier versions of themselves, in the following places: *Arc, Brick, Border Crossings, TOK, The Fiddlehead, Interim, Literary Review of Canada, Matrix, Riddle Fence,* and *The Walrus.* Thanks to the editors of each. And to the guest editors, Stephanie Bolster, A. F. Moritz, and Lorna Crozier, respectively, for including poems in *Best Canadian Poetry 2008, Best Canadian Poetry 2009,* and *Best Canadian Poetry 2010.*

The Canada Council for the Arts and The Ontario Arts Council provided assistance during the writing of this book. I am grateful to both, and to the participating publishers in the Writers' Reserve Program of The Ontario Arts Council.

To readers who gave of their time and attention at various stages, David O'Meara, Suzanne Buffam, Srikanth Reddy, Don McKay, and Kevin Connolly, profound thanks.

Bill Douglas. Melanie Little, Kelly Joseph, and everyone at Anansi, a bow to you.

John and Christine Repas, for joyous and devoted childcare.

Karen Solie, who guided the book through late stages with patience, severity, and a glowing intelligence.

Laura Repas. Better than the dreaming.

AUTHOR PHOTOGRAPH: CAROLIN SEELIGER

About the Author

KEN BABSTOCK is the author of three previous collections, *Mean*, *Days into Flatspin*, and *Airstream Land Yacht*, which was a finalist for the Griffin Poetry Prize, the Governor General's Literary Award, the Winterset Prize, and won the Trillium Book Award for Poetry. All three titles were selected as *Globe and Mail* Top 100 books. His poems have appeared in several languages and have been anthologized in Canada, the U.S., and Ireland, and most recently in *The Oxford Anthology of Canadian Literature in English* and *Best Canadian Poems* 2008, 2009, and 2010. Ken Babstock lives in Toronto.